FOR THE BIRDS

First published in 2023 by
The Dedalus Press
13 Moyclare Road
Baldoyle
Dublin D13 K1C2
Ireland

www.dedaluspress.com

Copyright © Victoria Melkovska, 2023

ISBN 9781915629111 (paperback)
ISBN 9781915629104 (hardback)

All rights reserved.
No part of this publication may be reproduced in any form
or by any means without the prior permission
of the publisher.

The moral rights of the author have been asserted.

Dedalus Press titles are available in Ireland
from Argosy Books (www.argosybooks.ie) and in the UK
from Inpress Books (www.inpressbooks.co.uk)

Cover image © Maryia Nenahliadava | Dreamstime.com
Three bird sketches in the text © Tetyana Tsaryk

Printed in Dublin by Print Dynamics.

The Dedalus Press receives financial assistance from
The Arts Council / An Chomhairle Ealaíon.

FOR THE BIRDS

Victoria Melkovska

DEDALUS PRESS

ACKNOWLEDGEMENTS

I thank my outstanding teachers and supporters, Mark Granier and Jean O'Brien, who lead the New Irish Communities writing group in the Irish Writers' Centre, for warmly receiving poets and writers for whom English is their second (or, in many cases, third) language. I am enormously thankful to the IWC for this opportunity, and for recognising the potential of diverse writers in the Irish literary landscape.

I'd like to express my deep appreciation to Yvonne Cullen, the steam locomotion of the Writing Train workshop, which pulled me out of dark times and enlightened me through many years of participation towards some writing successes, and now this poetry collection.

I am also grateful to the superb team at the Dedalus Press for making this book possible, particularly Pat Boran, for his professional expertise and attention to detail.

For the lovely interior illustrations, I am thankful to Tetiana Tsaryk, a Ukrainian artist who creates in Dublin.

My thanks, as ever, to my mother, for her endless support; my family for inspiring many of these poems; and my husband, Ciarán, for his love and for being my first reader and fan.

Finally, I would like to thank the Ukrainian Army for guarding the peace in Europe and the World during these tragic times.

Slava Ukraini!

Contents

Family Politics / 9

WE WERE FROM THE USSR

1955 / 13
False Pretences / 16
Snow Girl / 17
At the Beach / 19
Thieves / 21
Pilgrims / 24

NEW LAND, NEW HOME

Two Letters / 29
The Back Door / 33
Magnolia / 37
For the Birds / 38
Chinese Boxes / 41
Pegs / 42
Rooted / 43
Trick or Treat / 44
The Liberties, April 2020 / 45
Funeral FM / 46
Pre-loved / 48
Apple Charlotte / 50
Boy in a Blue T-Shirt / 51

Homecoming / 52
Equality / 53
Robin / 54
Kindness / 56
On finding a photograph,
where both of us have no hair / 57

WARZONE

Russians Came / 61
His is a Flowerbed Grave / 62
Necessities / 64
They Stare into Winter's Face / 68
Next to the Ladies / 70
Granny / 71
Yours Truly / 72

NOTES / 74

to Ciarán

Family Politics

My father's like Russia: strikes first.
Strikes hard. Strikes where it hurts. Strikes those
unable to answer either by word or sword.
Strikes those capitulating with pain –
amid pandemic, stroke or cancer.

Just like Ukraine, my mother has lost
her shores and weight. Bruises swell on her side,
and wounds bleed with shame. Unseen,
she cried the Black Sea until
her resilience changed her.

Like the United Nations' fist closing tight,
my brother and I don't stand with or by our father.
Aloof to saving his face imprinted on us,
we sink his ships, down his planes, destroy his tanks.
We grant him nothing but isolation.

WE WERE FROM THE USSR

1955

MAY:
For weeks the scorched soil
begs for a drop of rain.
A hoe and a shovel
in blistered hands
clash with the parched terrain.
Two sisters (the younger unkissed yet),
both exhausted but full of hope
bury the two-eyed baby potatoes
so later they'll harvest a crop.

A raven passes over the sun:
a raindrop, two more, and then – thunderstorm.
A flash!
       'Sister, run –'
A flash!
       'Grab the hoe –'
A flash!
       'To the ash tree –'
A flash!
'Give me your –'
Both drop to the ground.
Both are no more.

Charred, side by side,
cold and still,
found next morning
in the rain-scented field –
one yet to be wed,

and another
my future granny's
life-giving mother.

JUNE:
'... And your father?'
               'Another woman.'
'Who, then, looks after you?'
                She shrugs, 'Who?
                 Apparently, no one.
                      I do.'

Last night this blond, wide-shouldered lad
kissed a looker he only recently met.
Now he scratches the back of his head:
this one is sixteen, a short-sighted orphan,
has nought in the world, has no one;
the looker is proud of her folk and cows.
'Will you marry me?'
'When?' The orphan looks up.
And the answer is, 'Now.'

JULY:
It is for a month that they are wed:
my future grandmother and my future grandad.
And just as if they weren't a bride and a groom
they go to sleep in two different rooms,
shared with various roommates,
in separate buildings
on the opposite sides of war-wounded Kyiv.
They don't see each other sometimes for weeks,
so the marital bed neither rattles nor squeaks.

AUGUST:
'Mother planted potatoes before … you know.'
'If it's time to dig, then I guess we shall go.'
The roof is thatched, the floor mud-patched
in that sorry house where under the couch
shamelessly scratches a hungry mouse.
She pulls two pictures from under the cloth:
her mother, her aunt; she kisses them both.
A child with a wound so throbbing, so raw
she tries not to look at the shovel and hoe
tucked in the corner against the wall.
She's back home, now a woman, a wife
who came with her husband to gather
potatoes planted three months ago
by her then-alive mother.
They bake those spuds –
like the stove full of soot,
their bellies and hearts are full:
the potato crop appeared big,
enough to feed them and, maybe, a pig.
The raindrops thunder against the roof.
A howl outside, a distant 'Woof'.
A flash!
        And she jolts.
A flash!
        And she cries.
A flash!
          And he cuddles her, hums lullabies.
He holds her tight, and he keeps her warm.

NINE MONTHS LATER:
their daughter,
my mother, is born.

False Pretences

hold the hem of your new satin skirt,
lift it and stretch it –
like good girls do

pull back your shoulders, stop biting your lip,
smile, show your teeth –
like good girls do

write on the back *From Vika with love,*
date it and sign it –
like good girls do

I know I'm going to tear that photo: it doesn't ring true
oh, how I loathe striking a pose
like good girls do

Snow Girl

How old was I? No more than four or five.
My woollen scarf over my runny nose,
atop a sleigh behind my father's back
I'm pulled along the starry, frosty morning.

My dad's feet make the snow squeak and crunch,
a fox-fur hat is thick and muffles warnings
to hold onto the sides with all my might –
my gloves are caked and slippery with snow.

And I'm afraid. Afraid to tilt and fall,
be scolded for not doing what I'm told;
for being clumsy, making daddy stop,
and brush the snow off: he is late for work.

Or even worse, I am afraid to fall
unnoticed, be forgotten in the snow,
to miss hot milk with honey in pre-school,
and not just that: to miss the New Year show

in which I am to star as Snow Girl,
dressed in a shiny blue and white-trimmed coat.
Mom made it sparkle using just some glue
and prickly shards of ornaments that broke.

I am to hide in Witch's cardboard house
tucked right behind a ceiling-reaching tree
with lights and tinsel gleaming in its branches.
I'll wait till kids can come and rescue me.

To tell the truth, I don't mind – not a bit! –
sitting beside a sack with lollies, toffees,
waffles. I might allow my sneaky little hand
to take a lucky dip – and see what happens.

I know all the lines by heart by now;
what Bunny asks, what Squirrel says to Fox.
If they forget, I will be peacock-proud
to whisper hints from the safety of the box.

And if the Bunny-boy ignores my clues
his ample mom will come in leaps and bounds,
to grab his mask and press it to her face:
'I am a Runny Bunny!' like last year.

This makes me laugh inside the woollen scarf,
and when I laugh, it feels a little warmer.
But fingers numb with frost, as if not mine –
I lose my grip when Daddy turns a corner.

At the Beach

A sandy crescent by sloshy water:
the balmy weekend – a godsend.
In the shade of the apple tree
two of us, mother and daughter,
chitchat on the faded coverlet.

I lick the thick ice cream,
my mom's speckled hand
rubs my skin with sun-cream;
it tickles. We laugh and sing
A silly song
                            when
another mother – and son –
dock at the beach, nest nearby.
In the heat, in a town this small,
there is nowhere else to hide.

His mother, my mother,
they know each other:
under the tree, they chitchat
about jobs, friends and nemesis,
rising prices, medicines, recipes –
all that boring grown-up crap.

The boy is my classmate; he's eleven;
I'm ten. We share a desk in our class.
(Once, out of the blue, he nudged my braids,
called me names – I kicked him for that;
he nicked my eraser – I broke his pen.)
And now

                         this horror
of knowing your boobs are growing
and there's nothing to cover them with
but your hands. How unfair: this boy's
open stare – right there – no end …

I hug my knees, wondering what he sees
when I sit like this on my coverlet.
'Mommy, please, let's go into the water!'
(Why, oh why haven't you bought me
a boob-covering swimsuit yet?)

His mother slaps a mosquito, 'Hey kids,
why don't you grab your pool rings
and go swimming in the shallow water.'
He'll teach me to float on my back, he says.
(As if I'm mad enough to agree to that.)

I dart first to the river
to avoid the eyes of this dopey dreamer.
I'm an iceberg, my sunhat – its tip.
I won't turn to him, won't quit the water
until they went home.
Only, they never will.
Behind my back, there drifts his pool ring.
Above the river, his mom's awful scream,
and the warm unforgiving water.

Thieves

On our mom's 30th birthday
during a summertime break,
to surprise her I supposed
we could promptly redecorate.
In my mind, it was our granny's rug
(golden, low-pile) lacking
in our flat furnished in the Soviet style.
For a handful of toffees and mints,
my little brother followed me
to our grandparent's house –
twenty minutes away,
across the railway.

Short-cutting the rail crossing,
in the heat and the fuel odours,
little cheats we giggled and gossiped,
chewing and sucking sweets.
At our grandparents', no one was home –
the door was locked, a window was open –
we sneaked in, and the rest is history.

Voilà and *ta-da!* Look at us:
carrying home a massive rug.
It sagged in the middle, but
we felt so clever and smug
for pulling it swiftly from under
our granny and grandad.

Small hands aching and burning
with the bulky burden,

at the crossing, short-cutting again,
ponderous, we didn't notice a whistling and chugging,
charging at us – a cargo train.

The five-meter slug, with a kid on each side,
trying hotfoot to skip and run for our lives
across the rails, sleepers and gauges.
How the driver ever managed to stop
without killing silly us first?
He yelled and cursed,
and cursed and yelled –
our pants got hot and wet.

By the time our mommy
returned from work,
we'd washed ourselves
and made her a cake,
refurbished the living room,
sprayed around her floral perfume,
and last, but not least,
rolled out the Golden Fleece.

The telephone ruined the surprise.
Granny said, they couldn't come
to drink bubbly with us.
Their house seemed to be robbed,
the thieves escaping with the rug.
Guards were on the way
with a sniffer dog, Grandfather
was busy changing the lock.

When the truth crawled out,
we all laughed aloud,
picturing granny's shock.
To this day, old enough
to become grandparents ourselves,
my brother and I never share
the dread of the oncoming train.
The sound of its whistle,
our pants hot with pissing …
What were we thinking?
Listen,
  left and right,
listen,
  high and low:
there are frightful things
  mothers shouldn't know.

Pilgrims

1990: a train from Kyiv to Moscow,
a carriage that never airs,
the grey sheets that never feel dry.
We wait for departure in a stuffy compartment;
when the train jolts and pulls
we raise our feet off the floor for luck
and shout our goodbyes.

An hour later, our greasy fingers
tear apart roast chicken,
crack the eggshells, reach for a slice of rye
with smoked cheese. With such ease
my brother and I climb to the top bunks –
we're full of giggles, and the nuclear comebacks
of the lemonade fizz.

'Shush,' Granny whispers, 'Tomorrow –
imagine – tomorrow! – we'll see
the famous Red Square and the Kremlin
with our own eyes! And Lenin –
imagine – we'll see our Great Uncle Lenin!
Everyone must see the Kremlin and Lenin once!'

In the 2020s, how much there's left to remember?
In a photo, my brother back then – a stick-man
next to my purple parka and white winter shoes.
Moscow? Red Square? Thirty years ago?
All I remember is the queues.

A million-legged serpent creeps toward
its square-shaped, snow-covered head,
along the frost-hoarded Gorky Park. Sub-zero
miles, hours pass until the Kremlin's red star
dazzles us in the premature dark.

'Hungry, my dears? I'll get some sausages now,'
Granny leaves us to queue and runs to a nearby shop.
Her caring heart has neither suspicion nor clue
that while searching for food, she'll lose us instead.
And it will be a lamp-lit night, biting frost,
the Kremlin clock striking over our sobs
before we reunite in this human ant-colony crowd.

In the Mausoleum, I stare at how tiny great Lenin is,
at his waxy right hand (like a child's fist).
Granny squeezes my fingers. I know
she can't see him through the wailing wall
of self-blame and guilt, so I try
to remember for her all this, like a film.

We spot the next queue from a tourist bus.
A grumpy guide sneezes at us and points:
'The first McDonald's opened here last month,
right under the yellow M on the wall. Sorry,
behind the crowd, you won't spot the door.
When heading there, pack a sandwich with you:
people are left to starve in that monstrous queue.'
(Granny reaches again for a hankie.)

And I also remember a Ketchup Queue.
What was this 'ketchup'? We hardly knew
but still joined the fur-coated crowd.
Three bottles per person, so we got nine
and brought back home from Moscow some fine
crimson glass bottles in the blue net bags.
(O, that clink-clank as the train chugged home!)

A luxury foreign to Kyiv back then,
this ketchup (which Granny called 'keptcha')
we spread on sliced bread and invited guests
to taste the little red squares, fancy food of the era.
And I shamelessly nodded my braided head
when asked if in Moscow I was lucky to taste
A real Big Mac from McDonald's.

NEW LAND, NEW HOME

Two Letters

1.

Dear Grandad,
hope my letter finds you well
in that white-washed house
with roast pumpkin smell,
where you taught me
to count flies
in the frost-laced window.
It's been a year in a foreign land,
and now at last
I can honestly tell you
about my life in Ireland.

When I arrived in early spring,
the daffodil-scented air seemed so clean,
I swayed like a bar-fly around.
But that was before –
before I found
the tightly twisting roads,
the low-rise towns,
dog shit underfoot,
chewing gum on the ground,
and broken umbrellas trembling
in a bicycle lane.

Georgian terraces look the same;
the red-brick streets just differ in name.

And what would surprise you even more,
no one takes off their shoes indoors.
(The shoes, I admit, don't get dirty.)

My low-ceiling room has a musty stink,
a coin meter and a personal sink.
The taps are so short as if made for kids
to wriggle, for fun, their fingers.

The people, however,
that's a different story.
Simply put,
if you step on someone's foot,
you'd hear a humble 'Sorry';
a stranger would randomly say 'hello'
and thank a bus driver
(I wonder what for).
Yesterday,
running to my English class
I stopped when I heard laughter
at a funeral mass –
the Irish come to bid farewell,
often to near strangers.

Being devoted and feckless by turn,
they tuck into black buggies their new-borns.
Mum, insulated in a scarf and worn Uggs,
her baby, in a light frilled dress, barefoot
(or just with one sock, if lucky).

And the milky knees of Irish schoolgirls
flash all year round,
tremble like those umbrellas,
left to the mercy of wind.

Cafés put shutters down at seven, and
if I fancy meeting with a date or a friend
I enter a pub: noisy and smelly,
with the shouts and cries
and the blaring telly.
But, dear Grandad,
you mustn't fear:
I don't drink whiskey,
I don't drink beer;
I usually order black tea with milk;
white tea, the Irish call it.
I like it.

2.

Goodness, my dear,
What nonsense you've written here!
I utterly fail
to make of your letter head nor tail.
Please, fetch a pen
and write your answers:
How much is
salted herring (two ounces)?
How much money
you pay for a jar of three litres of honey?
What about other familiar goods:
ten eggs,
a bucket of rooster spuds;
a sack of sugar;
a loaf of rye bread.
I will decide
by knowing all that
whether your life in Ireland
is worth the ticket.

The Back Door

Traditionally, Ukrainian houses have only a front door

1.

Where I come from,
winter drowses on the window ledge,
scratching glass with bristle,
lies in wait for the slightest chance
to stick its foot in the door,
to slither inside,
twirl in for a second
and stay forever.
The leather-upholstered door
with a constellation of studs,
locked, latched,
chained like a dog,
guards
my childhood's Land of Plenty
against minus twenty.

2.

'If not for a random storm,
Irish winters are mild and warm.
Come to visit this Christmas,
mother.'
She sighs, 'Not this year. Another.'

3.

She comes;
gapes at the weird ensemble:
grass-covered lawns,
the cherry-tree blossoms fall,
a hare under a palm tree –
all in the midst of December.
But to her,
one thing
is the strangest of all.
Not my ceiling-mounted windows, no.
Not stepping on the pleasantly heated floor.
She wonders at something so trivial:
my back door.
And her fingers smelling of dill
tremble turning the key,
to let in
the thrush song,
as if winter,
left many miles away,
could catch on
and invite itself in.

4.

Back home,
I smile into a watermelon slice:
a bowl of raspberries on the ledge,
crispy apples, soft pears
just where the winter slept.
My son's honeyed kiss
lands on a pancake of his grandma's cheek.
A new back door to the garden swings
(letting in
the chirruping whirl,
the flies too,
the smell of barbecue)
and bangs behind him.

Magnolia

for Sophia

Pinkish magnolia petals dotted the ground –
footprints of the spring's little feet
running fast into the sunniest summer.
This morning my daughter tried on her shoes
stowed away just before the snowfall.
So light and so pretty, with the furry pompoms,
those shoes – what a pity – are now too small.

For the Birds

Evening chores: scrape the plates,
put the dishwasher on, and when it gurgles
bring the pieces of old toast and bread outside –
for the birds. I tell my kids,
'Even if it's stale, musty or dry
on a wintery morning tomorrow
our bread will be an early bird's find.'

A new day: the clank of the bowls and spoons;
fridge beeps, toaster pops, microwave hums.
And while spreading hot toast with rock-cold butter
we barely hear a thing,
neither cars nor chirp nor wing-flutter.

Kids crunch their cornflakes,
slurp milk from the spoons;
under the table – feet-fight.
Hugging a coffee mug,
I peep through the fairy lights
last night put over the window.

Outside, pigeons peck around the rowan tree,
safe on the path. For once,
the all-seeing seagulls
aren't first to spot the festive feast.
And in the steamy shower's warmth,
my heart sings a tune in a silly voice

when I think of birds feeding
and perhaps flying away

with a crumb in a beak – for a chick.
Do they even breed in the winter,
I wonder, brushing my teeth.

Ten to nine, our 'leaving-for-schoolie' time.
I turn the key, open the door, and let my little ones out.
Water sloshes in the beakers
tucked into the bright backpacks.
The remains of their tin foil-wrapped lunches
may come back yet (food for the birds).

Which are gone, except one:
a grey, red, white feathery blot on the roadside
imprinted on the asphalt,
pressed flat into the ground
by a wheel of a passing car.

'Mama, look,' my little boy whispers,
then sobs, 'A birdie's dead.'
'Because of you!' shouts his sister,
'Because of your bloody bread!'

And my heart goes, 'Shite, shite, shite.'
And my mouth staccatos, 'Right, right, right.'
And I usher them on fast, fast.
'We'll be late for school.' We go at last,

leaving behind what once was a bird
and what were once toast breadcrumbs.
The sky's crispy blue, auburn leaves rustle,
and we walk sad and silent along the Coombe.

Cars flying by; cold hands in my pockets shake.
How to go back in time? How to make
out of that grey-red-white feathery blot
once again –
                like a puzzle –
                              a hungry but living bird?

Chinese Boxes

Last April, this house went up for sale.
He came to the viewing and instantly knew:
a two-bed red brick in the old Liberties –
without a doubt meant to be his.

The box-room window facing the back
delighted his eye by the wide-view prospect:
a slice of a rainbow in the silver skyline,
a looming in the distance mountain pile.

And in his mind's eye (or just by default)
he thought from that window he could see it all:
furry fir trees, sheared sheep, golden gorse,
as he filled to the brim this room box by box.

Boxes bulging with wires, and books,
toolboxes with levels, screws, rusty hooks,
boxes of pictures, jackets and shoes,
boxes marked 'what-nots' and 'booze'.

Sorting them all did take him a while,
when, almost done, he rolled up the blind.
The mountains barred by new-build rental blocks.
He drew a gin bottle from the very last box.

'My view,' he said, his face ashen-pale.
Next morning, his gaff went up for sale.

Pegs

When we moved in, from the kitchen window,
there were rare featherless birds,
so tiny, curious, jazzy and cheerful,
resting on our washing line,
stretched across the subsiding lawn
from the house to the garage covered with ivy.
Were they checking our strength or the line's?
Their yellow, blue, pinkish beaks together
opened in a mute song, saluting the rising sun,
settling mist, a kissing breeze, a thunderstorm –
but they didn't come to visit for the weather.

As autumn puts her bright wellies on
making splashes in the muddy puddles,
as the wintry storms approach our home,
with Krispies and Frosties for breakfast,
I tend to dry my bed linen inside,
on the airer, watching my bird-pegs
unfed, swayed by the wind, refusing to fly,
holding tight to the frostbitten wash-line
with their faded beaks-turned-claws –
just like anyone grasping at straws.

Rooted

Next to the stone threshold
she buried
the shrivelled umbilical cord.

An apple sapling marked the spot –
her offspring
close to home.

A lifetime away, in spring,
I ache, tugged by that string
back
to apple blossom
at the stone threshold.

Trick or Treat

I see them across the road:
Vampire, Pirate and Toad.
Gawking, they grapple peanuts,
jellies and poisoned apples,
fill their bags with the offered fruits
of my lonely and grey-haired neighbours.
And the rain stripes the painted faces
designed to dismay.
Jack-o'-Lantern's grin
gives me eerie twitches:
not a culprit I am, just a witness,
a witness.
I spruce up the porch, vacuum
fallen leaves and bad dreams
woven from worries, and these
bespoke overnight cobwebs –
to replace them with fake ones.

The Liberties, April 2020

These budding branches right above,
this dazzling sunshine;
a guilty walk around my redbrick block –
I tread no further. A month or more
my neighbours wouldn't bother
with gauze curtains or blackout blinds.

The rowan crown's gossipy with songbirds.
The nosy parkers pry inside and tweet
among themselves the feather-raising news:
the humans are entrapped, encaged, endangered;
where lovers used to toss us crumbs,
the foxes play a ruse.

Do songbirds spot in one of those windows
a boy's foot slowly swaying side to side?
(His puffy toe just wriggled off a fly.)
He slouches on a couch with his phone.
A slanted shadow rests upon his face.
Sunbathing feet, why should he even know
the stranger sees him from the lonesome street.

Funeral FM

We reappear from the bowels of the Lidl car park,
from the gloom underground into the sun blast,
from the hiving anxiety into the street's eerie calm.
I press a button to open the window and gasp for breath.
You push a button to push my buttons
and switch on the radio, Funeral (fecking) FM.

Guilt-laden, I once confessed to a crime:
classical music was never a passion of mine.
Magical Mozart by Candlelight, high-pitched violin
Made you teary-eyed, tuned me up to leave …
Like balsamic and oil, our musical tastes didn't mix,
didn't blend. With one accord this was
something to fix, to lose, to end.

Now – apart from the soothing silence – our house
fills with orchids, bright cushions and piles and piles
of books. No other noises but dishes, showers,
children's voices, Lego clacking, the neighbour's puppy
yapping about its business, and the piano
we bought for Sophia (from Santa) last Christmas.

Your car is the cemetery where your classicals hide.
In jest, to annoy me, you free their ghosts as we drive
down Cork Street. Pious scores of the cellos and flutes
boil my blood, cramp my guts,
tighten my glutes, tense my body into a cat-string
to be sawn to shreds by the vicious cut-throat violins.

Can't we listen to dopey disco, hip-hop or glam rock?
No, suffer sonatas, cantatas and fugues, little children:
Handel, Rachmaninov, Bach,
(and not to forget Chopin!) So I ask you,
how to tell 'The Good Mourning Show'
From 'The Late Late Show' on Funeral (fecking) FM?

Poor you, bursting with giggles
just as the bags in the boot burst with provisions –
hand sanitisers, toilet rolls, meatballs, veggies, fruit …
Have we once again spent more than we should?
Did we once again buy more than we need?
Through the window, the wind ruffles your curls,
and my hand cups and squeezes your knee as we speed up.

Then, heartsore, for once I fall silent and swallow
my orders to keep your chamber orchestras out of town.
I don't jokingly clench my teeth any longer or curse.
Down barren Cork Street only two cars are driving:
ours
      and the one which we happened to follow –
                                      a hearse.

Pre-loved

A stroll through the blossoms of Sundrive Road,
a busker's sing-song, cosy coffee aroma –
I sip from a cup and mindlessly halt
to peer through the window of a charity shop.
My window-shopping policy's strong:
I want a well-ordered, moth-free home.

In the messy assemblage displayed, I magpie
a tarnished cookbook I'd happily buy,
a sparkling necklace – I mentally try it
against my fading-to-paleness skin
reflected in a skeletal white mannequin.
A dress pinned around it would suit me well
(cheap enough to try on, I'm telling myself).

Mother-moth, don't move in the folds. Sit still.
If your luck's in today, you probably will
nest your flickering self and three dozen eggs
in my house. So hush, watch my legs
crossing the woodworm-eaten threshold;
read my eyes smiling *hi* to a sulking salesgirl.

Behind the drape, I take off my garments –
worn runners, jeans and a cold-shoulder T.
Headfirst, I'm diving into this gown
and rise to the bait like a foolish fish.
When I re-appear, in the lake of the mirror
the penny drops: everything new is forgotten old.

Coffee-coloured, dotted with petals,
lace-layered by order of fickle fashion,
this dallying dress – just one of a million,
consigned to KonMari de-clutter oblivion
in a swirl of a spring-cleaning, joy-giving spree –
was pre-loved, packed away and donated –
                                            by me.

Apple Charlotte

The cinnamon smell wafts through the house,
in the oven again reigns your Apple Charlotte.
Whisk three eggs, a cup of sugar, and flour,
for a thick and smooth batter; cover
the diced apples dusted with spices. Give it an hour,
until you are happy with the hard golden crust.
Let your royal pie rest for some time in its hoop.
Clotted cream on the side, sugar-powdered crown,
you slice it and call, 'It's ready, my darlings!
Come downstairs and mention to Daddy
in our dated and warm kitchen parlour
her Majesty's waiting, the Queen's Apple Charlotte.'
But you know, their dad doesn't need to be told –
lured by the smells, he's already there in the hall.

Boy in a Blue T-Shirt

Chasing a ball on a verdant pitch,
rowdy, gangly, with milk moustaches,
schoolboys shake off beads of sweat
from sunburned foreheads.
Messy cowslicks, croaky voices, strong legs.
'Yay!
        It's a goal!
                What a shot!'
When I ask my son who scored,
he waves his hand, points,
       'That boy,
              in the blue T-shirt!'
And I search for a boy in blue,
while the team
raises up,
      rocks,
            hurrays its hero,
the only lad on the playing field
with black, almost purple skin;
just 'a boy in a blue T-shirt'
to my son and his soccer team.

Homecoming

Through the mist, misery, mystery
wrapped around the ruined monastery,
he comes back to his beloved Inishbofin,
lulled by the ocean in his shiny coffin.
Here are the fiddles, guitars and accordion
waiting to wake him, to welcome him home.
Brawny hands heave him up the pier,
not allowing the wind to part
his and the hands they used to shake
often and hard. To the graveyard
of sea-facing headstones, up the hill,
down the winding bramble road
sails his broken and silent heart
in his mastless boat.

Equality

We share a pair of swimming pool boobs,
my mother and I. We took the mastectomy route
together, one year of the Covid nightmare.

Both flat, we don't meddle with this or that
implant option; our chests refuse adoption
of skin and fat from the thigh, belly or back.

Sometimes, when the occasion calls,
when going for meals, to the pools, concert halls,
we stuff inserts into our bras and chat.

My mommy's eyes moisten when she recalls
herself as a young midwife returning to work
after my birth: her maternity leave was so short.

She put her milky, leaking boobs to good use
by nursing a foundling left in their department;
that chance wet nurse now succumbs to cancer.

After my operation, on the way from St. James's,
I said in jest, 'Hubby, fancy some chicken breast?'
And, putting a seat belt across my flat chest,

I finally felt his equal.

Robin

A day after she died,
a robin flew
into our garage.
It was the only time
when I thought
the old wives
might be right,
and their tall tales
true.

But then you
reminded me,
quelling laughter:
the old wives say
*If a living bird
is stuck inside,
someone in the family
will die soon,*
and the robin
came after.

An amber feather
caught in a cobweb,
2022,
13th Feb,
St. Valentine's Eve.
Now I have
a tale to retell,
and ashen hair

to hide. Darling,
don't look,
don't laugh:
before your eyes
I'm turning into
one of those
old wives.
I sense, that day,
she came
once again
to visit.

Kindness

It cost ninety-six euros
to stitch the torn neck
of a Polish chicken,
your new puppy's victim.

You didn't roll your eyes,
not thinking twice,
smiled at the vet,
paid the price.

Three years after,
the feather-head clucker
repays your kindness
with a warm free-range egg.

On finding a photograph, where both of us have no hair

I had to shave my head
when my locks, dyed blond,
began, like leaves, to fall
responding to chemo.
In the same picture,
you're leaning
towards my velvet chair
and laugh: almost no thatch,
because a new barber-girl
across the road
clipped it a little too much,
your greying, receding hair.

WARZONE

Russians Came

They crucified a dog on the door frame,
in blood-flooded butchered Bucha.
They murdered a thousand dolphins
that basked in the brooding Black Sea.

They stole raccoons and wolves from the zoo,
in God-forsaken, now re-taken Kherson.
At the herd of calves sleeping in stables
they threw a bomb.

They are puzzled why foreign flamingos
this summer visit the estuaries near Odesa
in salmon-pink flocks, amid the explosions
blasting the balmy, beach-friendly weather.

Why our watermelons have guts to ripen.
Why our sunflowers dare to blossom.
Why the ears of our wheat don't wilt.
Why our red-lipped girls are so awesome

And why their children don't cry but yell
from across and beyond Ukraine: Hey orcs,
we want to draw with bright chalk and play,
drink lemonade and eat honeycombs.

Russians, why, by the same way you came,
don't you all just fuck off home?

His is a Flowerbed Grave

He ran towards it, skipping steps –
from the top-floor flat,
just as he often did
      after his cat,
           to school,
                for bread
daily before the war.

He ran towards it – the air-raid siren
wailed a wake for him and his,
neighbours poured into the cellar
        to hide,
           to cry,
                to pray
together, for peace.

He ran towards it – no shoes on his feet,
big toe through a hole in his sock –
past what he loved best –
a redhead next door,
        a one-eyed kitten,
              his lop-eared friend –
all in pieces, but outwardly whole.

His is a headless body
among the apartment block's rubble,
wrapped in a black plastic bag.

His is the mother who tears a hole
in it with her teeth,
takes into hers his lifeless hand
             to stroke it,
                        to whisper,
                                   to shout
'Wake up, wake up, Artem!'

By his side day and night
with the sirens she cries
from sunrise to sunset.
Hers are the fingernails that save
               the sombre soil,
                         snowdrops,
                               and sorrow
of his hand-dug flowerbed grave.

Necessities

after Tim O'Brien

1.

The things they carried
were largely determined by necessity.
Among the necessities or near-necessities were:
rolled rugs, washing machines, a wicker chair,
hair dryers, nail polish, manicure sets,
bikes for boys, pink hair-pins for daughters,
squeaky toys and Pedigree packs for pets.
Sergeant X, a first-time father, carried a pair
of gold earrings smeared in blood. Devil may care
if the skeletal screaming thing was a teen.
He took her first, then her life, and, after, the token
for his sky-eyed, dimple-cheeked, spit-of-him toddler.
Major Y took as a keepsake a lacy thong –
to smell the hanged girl, taste her on his tongue
on the road retreating from Makariv to Mozyr.
Back home, his dearest banked on the branded trophies:
iPhone, Sony TV, Dior, Bosch, BMW, Audi –
the badges of honour for Putin's defender.
Before he was shot, Captain Z made a call.
He told what he saw in Ukraine: a mince-grinder.
His mother's voice on the other end enquired,
'Is there a blender?'

2.

The things they carried
were largely determined by necessity.
Among the necessities or near-necessities were:
passports, smartphones, photos of perished parents,
dog-eared euros, dollars and Polish money.
Their shabby backpacks filled with cans, tampons,
and granny's gold, to be sold in the land they'd reach –
fingers crossed – in a couple of days, maybe weeks.
Red-eyed, a mother carried a bundle of nappies;
her baby crying from teething, smiling at the puppies,
never steady, looking around high and low
for his rib-tickling (shot in the head) Daddy.
In the bright bags, tired and wrinkled,
bottled water from rusty taps and dirty snow
melted in the enamelled bathtubs just over a week ago.
A toothless maths teacher's rucksack smelled of rye
with butter. Jealous, she sniffed smoked salami packed
in a swanky suitcase of a chic hair-cutter, thinking,
How this ruthless war could solve such a bitter equation:
A bag plus a train to a foreign terrain equals evacuation.
A crowd plus a missile strike equals unspeakable sorrow.
Lost love, lost limb, lost luggage, lost life and plenty
of half-eaten apples, the nappies soaked in blood,
the buggy, silent and empty. On the other platform
a luggage mound, a pile shabby and shiny.
All those chequered sacks and ripped backpacks,
Vuittons stuffed with meatballs or salamis,
they still sing in a hundred ringtones –
name whichever you fancy. Only to none
no one would ever
answer.

3.

The things they carried
were largely determined by necessity.
Among the necessities or near-necessities were:
buckets of faeces carried out of the cellar,
blankets and shrouds (stained and smelly),
the decaying remains of those already gone.
Like this man who brought a scarf
so, if needed, at night, he could tie
his hands to a leaking waste pipe –
freeing space for young nursing mothers.
And as standing he slept, so standing he died
while the town was for a month occupied
by *rashists*. Like this granny, who carried a cat
and silently rocked him forth and back
to sleep or to death in a cellar-turned-shelter,
hiding from flying missiles. The cat
had nine lives, like little Alex,
who went grey overnight waking up
wrapped in the feel of his Mama's
last hug. Neighbours said, 'It's the hunger,'
and a monstrous bomb crater
swallowed her like a gross alligator. Her cross
was made of Dad's stolen BMW plates.
Inside Mama's emergency bag: candle stubs
wasted lighters and empty painkiller packs.
Alex carried all that to their two-bedroom flat –
or, rather, to what was left of it: no rugs,
no washing machine, no TV or phone,
Mama's hair dryer and the chair were gone,
as his football and BMX bike were gone,
and all the perfumes to remember her by,

and the runners Dad swapped for combat boots
gone missing. What was left was broken glass,
rotten food, vodka flasks, his torn copybooks.
By the graveside, stroking the meowing cat,
with the dead man's scarf around his neck,
Alex sits on the day he turns seven.
At the cross, he places all he could bring:
a tin of sardines someone handed to him –
so his mother will not starve
in heaven.

They Stare into Winter's Face

No fear in their eyes, just the reflection
of the birthday cake candles,
giving them scarce warmth and light.

Minus five outside, plus darkness;
divided between the four of them,
multiplied by their echoing laughter:

Count the candles, Aunty – eight!
They are from my last birthday cake,
but guess what? I am nine today!

On her tepid belly, day and night long,
under the blanket, to keep them warm,
my nephew's mom holds her newborn.

The baby hasn't been outside for months,
the tip of her nose never touched by sunlight,
her lullaby the air raid siren.

The ninth-floor window, missiles whistle,
the lift has been dead for eight weeks,
the pram is too heavy to bring up and down.

The endless blackouts and air strikes:
generators humming like mad beehives,
cellars and bathrooms are now bomb-shelters.

In sherpa jackets and woollen blankets,
the pale kids sit in front of the screens,
their dark apartments lost in the snowdrifts.

With sunrise, they study online in a rush:
their hair uncombed, teeth unbrushed.
They'll remember themselves like this forever.

They'll recall staring into Winter's face,
Growing resilient in wartime Ukraine.
General Frost, you've lost. Putin, capitulate!

Next to the Ladies

From the war zone, a soldier returns –
in a carriage peopled chiefly by ladies.
The ladies complain: their noses find
the soldier's odour, *eww,* so offensive.
All that he has are these off-duty ten days,
to use, as he pleases, his limbs and his life.
Next week, by the same rickety train,
he'll return to the trenches – maybe to die.
Does he mind?
Does he mind, as an officer and gentleman,
spending alone a floor one-night stand
in the vestibule, next to the 'ladies'?
Don't the 'ladies',
in his collateral-damaged mind,
trump the sordid and freezing trenches?

Granny

I haven't grieved for you yet.
I haven't got time for crying,
for holding the love you've blown
into my being while dying
miles, miles away. For a year

or so I swallowed my sorrow,
silently sipping on Irish cider.
Granny, I foolishly thought
you'd give me time to untie this knot
of my mother's cancer, virus, stroke,
and the perfect storm of your
Prodigal son deserting her.

Granny, I'm sorry to say I'm glad
you didn't live to learn of that,
and of the war, burning down
the cornfields and seas of sunflowers
we passed every year in summer,
driving to yours a van full of fun –
a laughing, light-hearted crowd.

Soft and dry, like your dumpling dough,
your hands worked on kneading us all
into shape. I'm your dumpling, your muffin,
Granny. And I'm proud to say, your wisdom,
your wayward word-weaving ways
are alive still: Granny, I keep them breathing.

Yours Truly

Made of dark chocolate,
cherries, sour and sweet,
of pickled ginger,
dreamy lavender tea,
made of printed pages,
highlighted to death,
made of C minor,
and mango sorbet;
of fine-tip notes
on index cards,
of unwritten poems
and telescope shards,
of the headphones
and big microphones,
of radio waves
resonating in bones;
made of deep cellos
and thoughtful oboe,
made of the colours
white, black and gold,
made of air-soft pink
and deep turquoise,
iced Pina Colada
and hot glue wines;
made of bath-bubbles
and yoga classes,
of poetry groups
and prose practice,

made of deadlines
both missed and met,
of 18th century
Lyon lace;
made of stucco
in Newman House,
made of tattoos
defining eyebrows;
of a carriage and six,
and a tall shipwreck,
Virgin Suicides flicks
dewy-eyed soundtrack;
of phantom pains
and macabre humour,
of nervous shakes,
triple-negative tumour,
of Byron's rhymes
and Cohen's songs,
of the bloody battles
for sunny Kherson;
of Kubrick's film
Barry Lyndon,
made of your rib –
(I'm looking at you, Ciarán),
of Gascony vineyards
and Gothenburg's *fika* –
made in Ukraine,
yours truly,
   Vika.

NOTES

Necessities, p. 13:
'Rashist' – from 'Russian' and 'fascist'; a common term in Ukraine for Russian troops.